salmonpoetry

Publishing Irish & International

Poetry Since 1981

where the lost things go
anne casey

Published in 2017 by
Salmon Poetry
Cliffs of Moher, County Clare, Ireland
Website: www.salmonpoetry.com
Email: info@salmonpoetry.com

ISBN 978-1-910669-90-7

COVER IMAGE: © *Cumypah | Dreamstime.com*
COVER DESIGN & TYPESETTING: *Siobhán Hutson*
Printed in Ireland by Sprint Print

*Salmon Poetry gratefully acknowledges the support of
The Arts Council / An Chomhairle Ealaoín*

"my prayers are prayers of earth's own clumsily striving
(finding and losing and laughing and crying) children
whose any sadness or joy is my grief or my gladness
around me surges a miracle of unceasing
birth and glory and death and resurrection:
over my sleeping self float flaming symbols
of hope, and i wake to a perfect patience of mountains"

e.e. cummings

Acknowledgements

Acknowledgements are due to the editors of the following publications in which some poems from this collection were first published:

"In memoriam II: The draper": *The Irish Times*, 31 January 2016.

"In memoriam VII: Abandoned": *Tales from the Forest*, Issue 3, 2016.

"Credos": *Tools for Solidarity* poetry pamphlet, June 2017.

"Denial": *Thank You for Swallowing*– special edition, 'Fear', Vol 2, Issue 3, 2016.

"Infusion": *Into the Void* magazine, Issue 2, October 2016.

"Correspondence": *Luminous Echoes: A Poetry Anthology*, January 2017.

"Smörgåsbord": *The Blue Nib*, March 2017.

"The unwelcome house guest": *The Blue Nib*, March 2017.

"Patina": *Deep Water Literary Journal*, Issue 1, February 2017.

"Inversion": *Dodging the Rain*, Issue 2, January 2017.

"Suspension": *Dodging the Rain*, Issue 2, January 2017.

"Metaphoric rise": *The Irish Times,* 20 January 2017.

"Peekaboo": *Dodging the Rain*, Issue 2, January 2017.

"No-one will hear": *ROPES Literary Journal* 2017 (25th edition).

"Lost in space": *The Blue Nib*, March 2017.

"Morning rush II": *Visual Verse: An Anthology of Art and Words*, Volume 3, Chapter 12.

"The Lady Angophora": *The Incubator*, Issue 12, April 2017.

"Grounded": *The Murmur Journal*, January 2017

"Days like today": *The Remembered Arts Journal*, December 2016.

"Christmas kisses": *The Irish Times*, 30 December 2016.

"In Memoriam I: Made In Miltown Malbay" was shortlisted for the Cúirt New Writing Poetry Prize 2017.

"In Memoriam III: On my word" was shortlisted for the Cúirt New Writing Poetry Prize 2017.

"Credos" was shortlisted for the Cúirt New Writing Poetry Prize 2017.

"In memoriam XI: Giving way" was shortlisted for the 2016 Fourth Annual Bangor Poetry Competition.

"In memoriam XIII: Afloat" was shortlisted for the 2016 Fourth Annual Bangor Poetry Competition.

For Mum and Dad,
always, forever, wherever

Contents

where the lost things go

we sat upon a golden bow
my little bird and I
indivisibly apart
we dived into the sky
and to the purple-hearted dark
an ocean we did cry
for all the lost things
gathered there
in rooms beyond the eye
the aie, the I, the eye

In memoriam I: Made in Miltown Malbay

Bright sparks drift and chase
Like fireflies in the smoky haze
White-hot rod dashes
Headlong into waiting pail
Spewing acrid clouds
That catch the throat

A nervous whinny
Calmed by a steadying palm
The air ajangle
With the clang
And clink and rasp
I am agasp

Hidden, forbidden
Spotted, hunted
Paradise lost!
Racing down Main Street
Heart hammering
Fast as my tiny feet

Up the lane
Senses searing, heart ablaze
Too young yet to reason out
This magnificent labour
Rendering artful craft
From crude resource

* * *

Half a lifetime later
Half a world away
Transfixed in that memory
I realise that I too
Was forged
In that lost place

In memoriam II: The draper

"The town is dead
Nothing but the wind
Howling down Main Street
And a calf bawling
Outside *The Fiddlers*"

My mother's words, not mine
In a letter, kept in a drawer
These long years
She had a way with words
My mother

That's why they came
The faithful of her following
Leaning in to her over the counter
For an encouraging word
Or the promise of a novena

Long before we had
Local radio
Our town had my mother
Harbinger of the death notices
And the funeral arrangements

Bestower of colloquial wisdom
Bearer of news on all things
Great and small
Who was home
And who hadn't come

Who had got the Civil Service job
And by what bit of pull
The Councillor's niece
Smug in her new navy suit
Oblivious to the circulating countersuit

"Would you ever think of coming home?"
Her words would catch me
Unawares
Lips poised at the edge
Of a steaming mug

Igniting a spitfire
Of resentment each time
Then draping me for days
I'd wear it like a horsehair shirt
All the way back

Until the sunshine and the hustle
Had worn it threadbare
This extra bit of baggage
In every emigrant's case
Their mother's broken heart

I never thought to ask her
"Would you want me to…?
So I could look out at the rain
Circumnavigating the empty street
And shiver at the wind
Whipping in under the door…?"

I don't miss that question now
On my annual pilgrimage 'home'
My father never asks it
Like me, I know he feels it
Hanging in the air
Alongside her absence

I miss my mother
And her way with words

In memoriam III: On my word

"I'll come back for you"
She'd whisper
Just before they fell asleep
Their circular skirts
Draped over a chair
Stilled now
After all their twirling

"As soon as I'm settled"
She'd promise
Home for the weekend
Her bag ready
For the midday bus
Back to Dublin

"When I finish college"
She swore
Back for the summer
Helping in the shop
One eye always
On the door

"Once I earn some money"
She vowed
Right before
She met her match
And was swept away
From all their plans

Of meeting handsome brothers
And settling
Side-by-side
In big houses
With matching gardens
And gifted children

But through the years
They never
Missed a day
Talking for hours
Their phone bills
A testament to their bond

And the endless cups of tea
Made between breaths
While dandling a baby
Or warming a bottle
Testing the milk
On the other's wrist

A chunk of Calvita
Cut to quiet
A marauding toddler
The perfect blonde girl
Smiling from the blue box
Mocking their reality

They knew each other's
Neighbours
Though they'd never met
And the local priest
With his rantings
Though he was a stranger

They ferried bundles of clothes
Back and forth
Through the years
They were made of sterner stuff
Though they never lost the trace
Of one or other's house

"We'll go away together"
When the kids
Are grown and gone
And we have time for ourselves
But the time never came
And then she was lost

A light went out the day she left
But six years to the day
From when she died
She came back
As sisters always do
A promise made to be kept

In memoriam IV: The lady in waiting

You'd find her sitting in the hall
Ramrod in her navy suit
Packed bag at her feet
An hour at least
Before the agreed departure

Twisting her lace-edged hanky
Around her index
Anxious to be gone
Goodbyes not her strong-suit
She'd seen enough of them

Navy was her concession
To forty years of haranguing
For her widow's black
Less of a compromise perhaps
Than a signal to others when to give up

But strong-willed as she was
It came from a stronger heart
She'd had need of it
Orphaned in her teens
Widowed with three under five

She took her tea black too
No butter on her bread
Though she could well afford it
Habits, she said, from the wartime
Or maybe silent marks of respect?

Quiet-spoken, but unafraid to stand up
For what she knew was right
After a father who risked his life
To shelter resisters
In The Struggles

A trait that has endured
Along with her love of dogs
A stray was never turned away
From any door of her bloodline
And never will be

In memoriam V: Lawful wedded

For fifty-three years
She combed his hair
She made his tea
And buttered his toast
He didn't need her to
She just wouldn't have it
Any other way

For fifty-three years
He held her coat
Brought round the car
And opened her door
She didn't need him to
He just wouldn't have it
Any other way

After he retired
She ferried cups of tea
To the little garage
At the end of the garden
Where he fixed old sports cars
That they drove around in
Like newly-weds

After he died
She became his ghost
Drifting through the house
But followed him not long after
Though they couldn't find a cause
He didn't need her to
She just wouldn't have it
Any other way

In memoriam VI: Collusion

Sharper than any movie scene
I see them standing there
In the dusky air
Cedar shavings
Curling round their shoes
This unlikely pair

The younger
Clean-shaven, upright
In his sharp-creased suit
Fatherless all his life
The older
Silver-whiskered, bowed
As the branches of an ancient tree
Clad, top-to-toe
In finest dust
Sonless with a silent wife

Swaddled in the scent
Of antique woods
And aromatic finishes
The chill air blanketed
In friendly conspiracy
Trading chronicles
Of small-town clashes
Enemy strike and counterinsurgency
Raising eyebrows
And the odd guffaw

Unbroken until
Oblivious to
The greater craft at work
My invisible explorations
Of this hand-honed world
Dislodged a plank
The sharp thwack

Discharging a summary scolding
Harried apologies
And we whipped away

* * *

Standing again
In my seven-year-old shoes
It seems
Unimaginable to me
That it has all now
Fallen to dust

In memoriam VII: Abandoned

A shower of small black stones
The daily toll
To keep the ghouls at bay

That nestled
Deathly still
Behind those rotting boards

Watching
As you passed
From dark and silent eyes

Sending you flying
On a windy day
With a wayward howl from that gaping maw

Even the
Hulking black birds
Quietened as they clawed its broken thatch

Forty years on
A once-cheery usurper stands in its place
Paying doleful tribute to its forbear's fate

In memoriam VIII: Rural economy

Flared nostrils float me
To the little glass pane
Smudged already with the prints
Of other tuppenny dreamers

There on the floured boards
Golden nuggets beyond our reach
Peppered with juicy delights
Ha'penny in my father's day

Inflation and deflation in our little town
Marked in equal measure
By the rise of a small, elusive
Wodge of sticky dough

In memoriam IX: Spilt milk

The smell of
Turning milk sitting
On a sunlit windowsill
In an earthen jug
Waiting to be poured
Into the softly expectant flour

The plump curds
Squishing up between
Her knowing fingers
A smile curling at
The corners of her
Gently sagging cheeks

A crinkle in her eyes
As she nods for me
To lift the heavy jug
The wobbly splosh of
Its thickened load
And away again

With those practiced hands
Lightly circling and scooping
Until the lumpy mess
Is miraculously transformed
And she marks it
With a cross

After all the white
Clouds settle
Bare oak wiped
Flagstones swept
The air aloft with
Insides-melting promise

We sit together
Seventy years apart
But thick as thieves
Never guessing
How I would later
Let her down

That awful moment
When my father
Came home so quiet
And told us "She's gone"
My heart rent at the length
Since I'd seen her

With just a wall between us
The smell of
Slightly souring milk
Now forever inseparable
From the belly-flipping
Churn of my guilt

In memoriam X: Going, going, gone

The air alive with a fleet of caps
Checkered, plain, tweed and plaid
Holey elbows held aloft
Fending off a day gone soft

Ragtag jackets tacked askance
Bunching over twine-tied pants
Dung-caked legs tucked in tops
Of persevering aul' Dunlops

A whistle, a whoop
Ropes whipped in a loop
A merciless bawl
Bulls by the wall

A huddle a-babble
A loggerheads rabble
The lash of a tongue
A strange sing-song

A spit and a slap
A smack on the back
A tag-eared wad
Seals the swop

A soft, pink nose
Led off on a rope
Eyes like globes
Laced with hope

An elbow, a knee
And down with me
Sucked in the stench
A stomach wrench

Reckless boots
And feckless hoofs
A grab at my hair
A-fly through the air

To his broad shoulder
"They nearly sold her!"
Cuts through the din
From my saviour's sideways grin

Hero with no licence
Long gone since
Windswept tile or vanished child
No match for his country wile

"Mother of the Divine...
We were out of our minds!
A kick in the head...
You'd be stone dead."

Crumpled frock
Once-white socks
Spattered brown
One fell down

"And where's the other?"
Probes my mother
Pursed with rue
A beloved red shoe

The sorry cost
Of getting lost
Town Square way
On a Fair Day

In memoriam XI: Giving way

Pelting down the hill
Hands in the wind
Heart flying out behind you
Like a kite

Praying that your feet
Won't lose the pedals
On the bumps
Or you'll miss the turn

Where the road splits
Down to the slipway
Or over the gravel
To the pile of bikes

Abandoned
For the hike
Across the clifftop
To Kerin's Hole

Down the winding steps
Weathered and beaten
From the elements
And too many eager feet

A jump off the end
Where the path fell away
A quick check
To see who's there

Then the teeter
On the edge
Suck in a breath
For the ice-cold dive

Down, down
Into the navy depths
Soundless but for
The rush of your heart

And the water-muffled
Laughter of children
Unleashed for the first
Swim of summer

Staying under
'Til your chest is burning
And you burst out
Gasping and gaping

At the welcome spectacle
The push-in for the unwary
The daredevil dives
Not an adult in sight

Scrabbling at the shale
Breaking off in shards
As you haul out
To take the plunge

Over and over
Never getting old
'Til the call would come
To head for home

Not a watch between us
But we knew full well
To be back in town
For the Angelus bell

* * *

The broken steps
Gave way last year
To perfectly squared
And spaced concrete

With a steel handrail
Time and tide outmatched
By a host of names
On a shiny plaque

In memoriam XII: Final restitution

Ring a ring a rosie
A field full of posies
Marking the mounds
Where the lost babes
Were found

Down by the river
Come unbidden shivers
Anguish has stained
Where the banished babes
Were laid

Round by the sacred well
Blessings having been withheld
In the dead of night
Their lifeless forms
Were hid from sight

Sweet little innocents
Torn from their mothers' limbs
Laid where the fairy curse
Might earn them
Eternal rest

Ring a ring a rosie
The lost babes are cosy
In their cradles primrose-crowned
A stone's throw
From 'holy' ground

In memoriam XIII: Afloat

The stink of old dogfish
Clamping my nose
And lurching my stomach
Swaying with the gentle
Rock of the deck
Blinking into the lash of salt-spray
After each pitch

And away they go
The ragged bits of rotting flesh
Swinging inside the open mouths
Of the cages my father
Spent the winter building
In between
Puffs of Sweet Afton

Away with a swift prayer
For a healthy haul
On the afternoon run home
And we're off again
Chugging out past
Carraig na Rón
Eyes peeled for a lucky break

A dark brown silky mound
With two huge round curious eyes
Peering out of the water
By the edge of the rocks
Or the swell of your heart
Following the sudden leap
Of three or four or five

Slender navy curves
Breaching the crests
Basking shark
Rolling in formation
Rhyme or reason
Known only
To themselves

Sitting up like Lord Muck
Behind the giant wooden wheel
My father's weathered hands
Finding mine from time to time
To subconsciously correct
A wayward course
The subsea terrain laid out in his head

In my mind's eye
The sun forever shining
Though I know it wasn't always
Glinting off the soft inky crests
Turquoise melting into royal blue
Swirling into navy-black
Floating out of deepest green

And then we're round
The back of Mutton Island
Hauling up the nets
And the boxes are suddenly hopping
With the flickering silver
Blue and black
Of mackerel flipping front to back

And you're dog-tired
Pulling into the pier
The banter of the lads
Gutting and hosing
Letting fly a claw
A few faces gone now
One or two lost to the sea too soon

Up since four
But you'd be nowhere else on earth
Seafield pier on a summer's evening
Your mind already tasting
The panful of fresh mackerel
Dipped in salted flour
And sizzling in hot melted butter

In memoriam XIV: Plus ça change

You could set your clock by it
As the last gong of the Angelus bell
Reverberated out

There in spectacular tones
Of wriggling grey and black
Would be the little Petri dishes

As closely resembling
Your beans on toast
As scientifically possible

For round worms, fluke worms
Liver worms and tape worms
Sandwiched

Between the hour of benediction
And the aftermath
Of sectarian violence

In Belfast on the 6 o'clock news
A nine year-old boy hit in the head
With a stray plastic bullet

And you're scraping the last of the
Dripping beans onto your soggy crust
Trying not to think of brains

The '70s, challenging times
To sit down to your tea
In any rural Irish household

The horror these days
More evenly spread
Seemingly impervious to time and place

In memoriam XV: Dancing in the moonlight

It wasn't me he saw
When he held my waist and said
I will come for you at midnight
Listen for the tap, tap, tap at your window
It wasn't me entranced at ten
It wasn't me spooked at sixteen
It wasn't me able at twenty
To brush him off like all the others
It wasn't me he promised
To take dancing in the moonlight
It was the girl who said his name
Just like his mother had
Before she tied a tear-stained
Luggage-tag to his lapel-button
Blurring the words
No-one could understand
When he landed so far away
It was the girl he twirled
In the moonlight
Gently holding her waist
Crooning to her the lullaby
His mother had waltzed him to
Notes he hummed
Through all the years
Even long after
His mind went dancing

Credos

A penny in a new purse
(That it may never be empty)
The Child of Prague left out all night
(To bring a dry day for the First Holy Communion)
Never pick a flower from a fairy fort
(It will bring down a curse)
Never speak ill of the dead
(No matter how wicked they were, God rest their immortal soul)
A spit on the hand to seal the deal
A prayer to St Anthony to find something lost
To St Jude in the case of lost hope
Novenas on your knees if there's no hope at all
(Because miracles can happen – just look at Auntie Marie's
    neighbour's first cousin)
Never open an umbrella in the house
(It will stunt your growth)
Eat your crusts
(They'll make your hair curl, or straight if it's curly)
Don't make that face
(If the wind turns, you'll be stuck with it)
Red and green should never be seen
Never wear shiny shoes with a skirt
Only eat pork if there's an 'r' in the month
Don't change a clout till May is out
Waste not, want not
Never gift a knife to a friend
(It will cut your ties)
If a coal falls from the fire, a stranger is coming
Don't believe everything you hear
Seeing is believing

The rules we lived by
Before we had internet or mobile phones or colour tv
Before we knew
For better or worse
That no matter how complicated it might have seemed
Life would never be that simple
Ever again

Because
The wind *did* turn
Leaving us to face the ugliness
And the rain came down
The wicked were blessed
Hope was lost
Our growth stunted
Our hair curled and uncurled
As colours clashed
And on reflection
A strange underbelly was revealed
We consumed in excess
When we knew it was wrong
Changing everything
Piling wasteful want
Onto wanton waste
Knives out
Ties cut
Sparks flew
Strangers fell
As we followed the herd
Saw too much
Believed too well

So I am turning back
To times past
When all was lost
And my novena is this
Today, just for today
Let everyone
In the whole wide world
Wake
With eyes coloured
Only by love
With hands and minds
Able
Only to be kind

Because miracles can happen
Still

Open letter I: Dear Father

You stand there
In your robes
And pontificate

I sit here
In my Sunday best
Mystified

Willing the epiphany
Till one of the kids
Distracts me

And I miss the punchline
"Holy God"
I pray

Then you say
"Lift up your hearts"
And I do

Though
I only have
Just the one

And then
You get to
The Good Bit

And you have us all
Eating out of the palm
Of your hand

Open letter II: Dear Jack

Before you were born
I wanted to knock
All the sharp corners
Off the world

Smooth every stone
Pave every path
With pillows
Warm every cold place

How could I have known
As you nestled softly
Rising and falling
With my breath

How able would be
Those elbows
That protruded
Under my ribs

How strong
Those legs
That would carry you
Away from me too fast

Before you were born
How could I have known
How much
I had yet to learn?

Open letter III: Dear Joe

I gave you life
You gave me
A crumpled daisy
From your clammy fist

I gave you new clothes
You gave me
Cicada skins
And dragonfly wings

I gave you a feast fit for a king
You gave me
A scrunched-up sweet wrapper
And some bits of sticks

I gave you a cosy bed
You gave me
Sleepless nights
And broken dreams

I gave you comfort
You gave me
Countless nameless worries
And my greatest fears

I gave you life
And you gave me the world
Freshly sprinkled with fairy dust
And smothered in sticky kisses

Open letter IV: Dear children

I am sorry
For the world
I have brought you into

I am not
The driver of trucks or the
Puller of triggers

But I may
As well be
I hold myself accountable

As a 'responsible adult'
In our society
I must have failed

If the horrors
We witness on a daily basis
Prevail

If I have closed my eyes
To the unspeakable
Things

If I have voted in leaders who
Fail to seek human solutions
To human problems

If I have aided and abetted
The poisoning of our
Precious planet

Where the power of the individual
Has somehow surmounted
The common good

You make me want to believe
In a world that can
Heal

But for all the world I cannot
Figure out how to start
To set it right

Someone else's business

I

Leaving the blessed well
My grandmother already sitting in
The silver Spitfire so lovingly restored
By my grandfather's hands
Now holding his seat
Reaching for me

And I, wrenched backward
By a wracking keen from
Beneath the little stone bridge
A black and white collie
Desperately dragging at a sinking sack
Familiar hands gently pulling me back

"Come away *a leanbh* – that is
Someone else's business"

II

Looking down at these hands
That once were eight
Their lines and veins telling tales
Of how they have held
And gently pulled at
Their own protégés

Shielding eyes and covering ears
But never erasing the memories
And my heart drops
Like a stone-weighed sack
A hand-hewn stone, a small limp form
In a makeshift tomb

This sinking truth
The heart always knows
What the hands are doing

Growing pains

Midnight beckons
On the younger's first sleepover
Dragging my heart through the dark

Morning flight

Flying down the stairs
At nine or ten
I got a little
Ahead of myself

And was struck
That I belong to
No body
But I worried

For my lost self
Racing off
Without me
So I caught up

All these years later
From time to time
I have cause
To wonder

How many are there?
How many bodies
With beating hearts
And rushing, red blood

Filled with ideas
And desires
All those arms and legs
Gadding about

With no souls

Denial

You are not the serpent
You are its coiled stealth

You are not its fangs
You are their sharpness

You are not the venom
You are its toxicity

You are not its strike
You are the millisecond before its impact

You are not malice
You are the absolute absence of empathy

I do not hate you
I fear you

I do not shun you
I deny your existence

Over and over and over

Infusion

Fear is black and yellow
Since the banded sea-snake
Face-to-face, round a rock
Too far from shore

And anger is electric blue
Slashed with Ferrari red
Bright as tomato sauce
I've forgotten why

Love is delicate eggshell pink
Like the cheeks of my children
Always smelling of vanilla
And impossibly kissable

Stress is black
Too matt to find dimension
Like a black hole
Collapsing you from the inside

And happiness is a rainbow blur
Fields in early evening summer
Chasing butterflies and running till
You fall down laughing in the long grass

Sadness is eggplant
(AKA aubergine), marooned in mauve
But fear, fear is always black and yellow
Fangs in your face, no ground under you to run

Correspondence

I leave it there
For a while
Like some jagged thing
Until foolish hope
Overcomes hollow experience

And I am told
That the beating heart
I stuffed with the unbroken spiral
Of a small, round apple
And glazed all over
With dark, sticky blood
Was not quite right

I leave it again
Until I tire of the tiny nicks
Each time I pass it by
Then reconcile it
To the rejection heap
Along with the others
That also taught me nothing

And I take up my blade

If you say so

Time to put that behind you now you say
As if my tongue had not turned to scorched stone
In the arid desert of my mouth
As if there was any inner dialogue
In the crashing tempest of my brain
A ready emergency brake
For the runaway train disrailing in my chest
Its piston engine hammering at breaking point
As if I could corral the swarming man o'war
That have swept away with my legs
Pull the pin at will on my jackhammer hands
Pour soothing salve over the strangled ropes of my throat

Sure I rasp
Give me a minute
And I'll pull myself together

Insomnia

The rubber seal
Had gone
Around the rim

She'd shut it tight
But light
Kept stealing in

And though she swore
She's seen to it
Before

The faintest hum
Now hinted at
A slightly open door

Smörgåsbord

Cannibals eating away at themselves
Feeding off each other
They'll consume you too, if you let them
Chew you up and spit you out
If they don't swallow you whole

Thieves in the night
Daylight robbers
It's not the cat that's
Got your tongue
It's indignation

Wonder widens your eyes
Despair shuts them
And while they're closed
Love plucks them
Right out of your head

Abhorrence freezes your heart
Empathy melts it
But callousness hardens it
Until anguish comes and smashes it
Into a thousand sharp shards

Fear picks one piece
And with skilful precision
Surgically excises your dripping spleen
To be served rare
With a fine Chianti

While panic is
Transplanting a lily
In place of your liver
Envy eats the remains
Of your shattered heart

So you'll no longer feel
When horror cuts the legs
Out from under you
Not to worry
Apathy will tidy up when they're finished

Made

They follow me sometimes
The ones in the shadows
The ones I hear
But never see

The ones who
Scurry
Softly scattering
When I look

Over my shoulder
Where they came from
Before

Before
I was made
Afraid

The unwelcome house guest

He appeared to take an unseemly pleasure
In the uncertainty surrounding his arrival
At times, turning up entirely unannounced
Others leaving you hanging for days, or months at a pinch

Irrespective of ambush or extended anticipation
You could never be fully prepared
Transfixed the moment
His shadow crossed the threshold

Even the counterpane in the guest room seemed
To stiffen at the abruptness of his presence
His rigid deportment cutting off all attempts
At cordial communication, once instated he would

Leave you to grapple with a flurry of hastily planned tasks
Their dispatch stayed until his visitation was set in stone
Overwhelm staved only by the unavoidable string
Of awkward social gatherings his stilted attendance demanded

Any half-hearted departure from his prescriptive specifications
Falling on deaf ears, his dominion stretching as far as apparel
Even the catering arrangements submitted to his sombre tastes
His more carnal appetites heedless of age or gender

He would pin you like some specimen awaiting his inspection
In some quiet corner away from the crowd
His rank breath and sickly cologne cloying your airways
Breaching your chest and curling through your viscera

His singular aroma seeming to linger long after he had gone
As if hinting at the possibility of some unexpected return
Though it was sure to be a cold and humourless affair
The unsettled air left hanging far too long

After death comes to call

Patina

I feel them everywhere
The ones who left

The thin boy shivering
In the dark cupboard upstairs
When I reach
To put away the towels

The strange fruit swinging
Inside the wardrobe I avoid
That wasn't even there
When they came

They find me
In dark places
Slipping in
Seeking out

The bride in anglaise lace
All aglow at the altar
Who followed me home
To show her blooming bruises

And her crushed throat
Such small hands
So white and hopeful
Wanting to be touched

Gently
Yearning for
A soul to see them
For who they would have been

I feel them everywhere
The ones who left

A piece of themselves behind

Metaphoric rise

A brief history of incidents surrounding the American
Presidential Election & Inauguration 2016–2017

ROUSTING

hot wind howls through a hollow log
tawny tumbleweed trundles
over downtrodden plains

August 2016

RAVENING

on a sunlit lawn
a plump slug streaks forward
eyes on stalks

September 2016

A NEW RELIGION

branches bowed with bloated fruit
nod to the gilded idol
dark clouds fall in behind

October 2016

AFTERMATH

a squat lizard basks
on a sickle-hacked trail
black legs flail from his lips

November 2016

IN THE BAY

beacon dimmed and tablet fractured
the lady endures
her robes about her feet

December 2016

PARADOX LOST

a fiery sunrise
heralds stormy days to come
ice shifts at the poles

20 January 2017

Up next

Trapped behind glass
paused in this unreeling
unreality show
Frozen before our screens
silent screams
at the unfolding parody
Fumbling for the lost controls
Where is the stop
rewind
delete
for this obscene pantomime?
Fast forward four years
Where will we be?
Some post-apocalyptic
unintentioned horror show
halfway between *Fox News*
and *The Hunger Games*?

What hope?

when the solution for the 'horrific torture' of two students
is 155 years behind bars
when a judge can find 'nothing redeeming'
in a human being
when the daily assault on our senses
is a senseless parade
slowly simmering our sensitivity
in a melting pot of poor choices
from Netflix to newsreels
streaming a steaming tirade of
violence spilling over the edges
of everything
when each day I repeat the same phrases
to my children of ten and eleven
to explain why I'm the only parent
rejecting requests for them
to join online
the stranger-danger-gamers
bullet-raking their virtual presents
perhaps
laying the traps
to detonate their actual futures
when a six year-old thinks
it was ninjas he witnessed
mowing down his parents
in their own home
what hope
what hope
what hope
for the ones in the womb
tadpoles waiting to be born
into the boiling cauldron

Peekaboo

I see you
Dusky eyes twinkling
Towards the sky
I see you
Lips curling up
No matter why

I see you
Cornflower blue dress
Hitched to help you run
I see you
Racing through the
Late morning hum

I see you
Tiny arm folding
At the elbow
I see you
Face tilting to the
Yellow glow

I see you
However hard
I try
I see you
Dusky eyes twinkling
Towards the sky

I see you
Splayed
Beneath the blue
That rained down
Hell on you

I see you

No-one will hear

Why do they want to put us in driverless cars
With 200 victims of flash-floods in Qatar
And the overgrown toddler taking over the planet
Clutching his crayons to scribble out
Civilisation drawn from the hearts and minds
And multi-coloured blood of better women and men
On whose heads he would stamp his shams

I like the space between my heart and the steering wheel
Where I can hold your first smile after waking
And cherish again the jagged hearts achingly
Painstakingly scissored, bestowed like a trophy
Where my soul can turn over the last beat of the moth
Caught in the updraught as we
Swooped out of the house

Stirring the spectre that the gaps started to shrivel and die
As we first reconciled to the piles
Of mobile devices with always-on wifi
The clatter of apps mandating the pace of each breath between steps
Measured and pressured and metred-out reps
The counting of blips between blinks
Sifting and shifting and shrinking our thinking
Prescribing our liking
Mining, divining, refining
Terrabyting the spaces to nothing

I don't want to be put in a driverless car
My brain instantaneously clamped in VR
Auto-conveyed between points in time
Each moment consumed to the millisecond
Optimised, proselytised, visualised, ritualised, perpetualised,
    immortalised
Apprehended, suspended in splendid isolation
Where I can't even hum to my own inner drum
And there are no more spaces between things
So no-one will hear me screaming
Ö

Red hot sting

I felt it all the way
no pain, just the icky press and separate
as my flesh gave way
all seven layers to the
razor-sharp scalpel
two minutes of cutting
shaking and trying to breathe
then the pushing and tugging
and there he was aloft under the light
my soul reached up to hold him
all slimed chalky white and bright, bright red

but black fell down sickly stealing our first meeting
steel wool filling my throat and ears
awakened by my body thrashing
and lashing itself
off the metal table, rebelling against the invasion
rushed voices, golf stories giving way
to a strange spewing of ccs and pressures
and then I'm sailing on a crashing sea
shuddering uncontrollably
floating under swimming lights
into an alien lab
planted with human heads strung with wires
atop rolling white waves, watched by small, round, winking eyes

embracing him later in a daze
the red-hot horror of the aftermath mangled up in new love
nestled next to me in the soft white clouds
then the rip and scream
and I'm the lady sawn in half at the circus
but without the magic
clasping the creeping rose at my middle
a pale-faced aide leaving me holding my two halves together
trying not to let escape the dark crimson slithering thing I fear
might be my liver

"you've ruptured" says the nurse from Waterford
what felt like hours later
letting it slip into a kidney dish
the paradox lost somewhere in my state of mind

a nurse from Waterford, turned reiki healer, later told me
I hadn't let go
that's why I had failed
in the way it happens
the switchblade wounds of women's tongues
stinging more than any surgeon's knife
salved over and over by my children's laughter
I saw on Facebook years later
that she had a son
I wonder if she birthed him standing in a field
then walked away into the sunset clutching her prize
a cherry-bright stripe glistening on her forehead

Lost and found

I hadn't a clue where I'd left it lying
A coat of champions it had been one time
But its days were numbered, if truth be told
It weighed like an anchor and was getting quite old

Its world-weariness chafed round the back of my neck
But loyalty whispered I should just give a check
I was left by myself to delve for awhile
Through life's lost threads heaped in a forgotten pile

There were top hats and tails brim-filled with ambition
Cloth caps and tweeds of humbler disposition
Umbrellas and stoles screaming hoi polloi
A necklace that twinkled with beads of joy

A shirt stained with guilt in a battered old case
Prudence and virtue embroidered in lace
A bracelet that glittered with bitterest tears
A filigree choker fastened with fears

I rummaged and dug, drawn to this or that
Until I was struck by a kind of small hat
A piece of black felt crowned with feathers of hope
One a bit banjaxed, a soft lining of taupe

With a comb of bent plastic which was missing some teeth
That I pried with a beam from the last of the heap
"Found what you lost?" floated over the stack
I smiled and I nodded and I never looked back

Lost in space

It should have been raining buckets
But it was a dry, grey day

It should have been biting cold
But the morning chill lacked teeth

I should have been shrieking like a banshee
But I was silent as a grave

My heart should have stopped beating
But instead, it blundered on

The walls should have fallen in
But they stubbornly stood their ground

I should have chased down your taxi
But I was welded to the spot

Peering out the window
Willing you

To not
Be gone

A last-ditch dash
Too late

To tell you
This simple eternal truth

Without you
I am

The dark side
Of the moon

If you're lucky

once I was seven years old
and the world seemed an awful big place
then I was seventeen and I went out to knock it into shape

climbed up high on an elephant in the jungle
held on tight as it took a fit and ran off
cowabunga!
watched day turn to night as bats stormed the sky
in Sumatra
waded to my waist in an afternoon monsoon
on the streets of Bangkok
found myself penniless and ripped off
in Hong Kong

leaped into a void miles underground
ran off a mountain with some wings on
ate the leg of a cat (don't judge me for that)
climbed a gigantic glacier
saw my guide disappear in a fissure
found the meaning of life in sunset on a beach in Seafield
witnessed the sun rise from the rim of a volcano that was live
viewed myself through the eyes of an orangutan in the wild
while she clung on to her child

nearly drowned once or twice, saw things clearly
against the odds, saved two times by Eilish Cleary
carried off in Istanbul by a Turkish charmer
held to ransom in the deep dark of Java
thought I'd go home for a while
and was mugged for the eighth time
with a razor in Parnell Square
in the heat of the moment, taking chase
bloody stupid!

but if you're lucky then you live and maybe you learn
as I did that you don't die, but you're reborn, when you give birth

how you multiply this mystic thing that is love just by giving
    it away
that there's a time to hang on and a time to give way
sometimes you've got to get lost to be found
take a leap to find your feet
slips you should never repeat
so it's twenty-seven years
since I ate meat

and we're all just specks
floating in space
clinging to the face
of this rotating clock
ticking through the frames
of a never-ending universe
there's no stopping it or
going in reverse
so it's good to remember that

once
you were seven years old
and the world's still an awful
big place

Perspective

Reflecting in the long grass
The pink and peach and lavender
Of a glorious sunset
Akin to a little broken thing
Caked with grime
But somehow undulled

Spit and polish and a bit of grit
Restored its full transparency
And peering through
With its rosy tinge
I walked out into the twilight
Of a world transformed

But darkness fell
With the finding that my prize
Was easily misplaced
Stowing it in an inner pocket didn't work
Events and incidents
Sweeping it out of reach

Like the unexpected finger
From the father in the flash car
Exiting the posh school at the top of our road
Money apparently having bought him
The right to cut me off
But sadly, not the price of his own happiness

That could be found for free in the long grass
Glinting out of the grime
This precious thing that could be
The saving of us all
If only we had 7.34 billion of them
A little lens of love for everyone

Morning rush I

Shambling down the suburban street
Oblivious to the buses
Hustling past
Lived-in track-pants
Tucked into odd socks
Poking out of broken slippers

A beanie trying to escape
Oddly scrunched
With a wayward seam
Making corners
Where they didn't belong
Above an angelic half-smile

He made no sense
Shuffling between
The tight-faced commuters
The clusters
Of school-kids elbowing
And thumbing their phones

And I wondered
After we'd passed
If it was just me
My subconscious out for a stroll
All at odds
With the world and its ways

Morning rush II

Every morning
I stand
Before my canvas
And I roll my eyes
At all the truths and tells

Reading between
The lines
The shadows
Veins
And blotches

And I set to work
Dabbing
And smearing
Sighing
And concealing

Every morning
I stand
Before her and
She smiles back at me
My Mona Lisa

With all her secrets

Morning rush III

Two birds on a wire
Looking down
"You cut me off!"
Beep, beep
"Mate, you're holding
Everyone up!"

"This guy pulled
Straight out in front of me!
I'm not taking this."
Beep, beep
"I'll be late for work."
"School starts in ten minutes."

"There goes my bus!"
"Come on mate.
Move out of the road.
Everyone needs to get going".
Beep, beep
"I'm taking your number!"

And away they went
The red-faced man
In the little red car
The mother and kids
With the husband
Who'd missed his bus

The eye-roller
In the shiny sports car
The string of
Cross-looking drivers
In a noisy line behind
And the birds

Kept looking down

Known associate

Unholy herald
Silent witness
Unshakeable disciple
Zealous missionary
Sneak thief
Fearless ally
Fervent waiter
Guilt tripper
Present bringer
Feckless destroyer
Wide-eyed believer
Faith healer
Committed decadent
Dishevelled angel
Heaven sent

Astir

parched bark flakes
from a sun-baked trunk
a chrysalis wakes

The Lady Angophora

golden limbs stretching
in the warm sun – winter garb
strewn about her feet

Grounded

He looks me square in the eye unflinching
Cocksure I will do him no harm
I envy his instinct for who might do him wrong
He reminds me I once had it
Until I let convention and politeness
Silence my inner voice

He displays himself for me
Basking in my admiration of his beauty
I envy him his swagger
He reminds me I once had it
Until I let it be crushed underfoot
By too many willing boots

He cocks his head and looks into my soul
Allowing me to capture a likeness of his
Something to hold after
And ponder his unique luminescence
Likely to long outlive
My own flickering glimmer

His interest extinguished
He lifts a limb
And unfolds his immaculate plumage
To conquer the suspended blue
I watch until his sulphur crown disappears
Behind the highest tips of the golden wattle blossoms

I envy him his wings

Palm Cove parade

Marching past the wedding couple
Simpering and struggling in the sand
For their troupe of photographers
Who outnumber their guests

Owl-eyed, straw-legged, sleek-headed
Swanning down the main drag
Stopping traffic
Like a flurry of supermodels

Animal awareness set on high
Observing their observers
Alongside the knots of legs
And the muslin-draped pram

Skirting the flapping toddler
Necks braced elbows akimbo
Stone-curlews ready to cast themselves
Into the sodden late afternoon air

Crepuscular stirrings

I have fallen down the rabbit-hole
and there's no way back
I am down here
with the scuttling things
scrabbling in the dark
between the tree-roots
throbbing with the music
of the soil
skitterings and scatterings
smatterings of secrets
I am starting to
tune
in
in
my stumblings
to
the rumblings
to
the patterns they are weaving
continuously
sinuously sifting
through the debris and
detritus of our spoiled lives
leeching from the surface
through the layers
to be shared
ingested and processed
compressed and regressed
miraculously cleansed
and I sense
a humbling
in the bumblings
but beware
the underdwellers dare
to prophesy
while humanity's

profanity
heaps more humans on the piles
a philosophy is thriving
in the hiving
from empty skulls
will be hulled
lullabies for survivors
of the netherworld reprisals
shush now
the humus is humming
and I'm slumming with the
thrivers
I have joined
the underground resistance
and confess I lied
I didn't fall
down the rabbit-hole
at all
I swan
-dived

Days like today

I am not old but I am worn down and frayed at the edges
And I wonder at what age will I say
Take me away
Let me shed my skin
Release all my atoms
Let them fall apart still sparking

Show me the place where they can separate
And stop their spinning
De-fused, diffuse, drift off
Sink into the moist earth
Seep into the pulsing womb
Where bandicoots probe while we sleep

Soil-dappled snouts carrying bits of me
Away under the dark branches
Glinting with the watchful eyes of possums
Strung with the spectres of escaped cicadas
Show me where there will be no more
Aching bones and world weariness

Where I can gladly give up my ghost

Between ebb and flow

Mist rolls off moss-green hills
Where wind-wild ponies thunder
Manes flying as they chase
Their seaward brothers
Locked in eternal contest
On this deserted grey mile

Past the little stone churchyard
Long-forgotten graves spilling
Stones onto the sodden bog
A soft snore from behind
My two angels sleeping
Thirteen thousand miles

From all they have ever known
Running our own race
To make the best
Of spaces like this
A rainbow rises along the horizon
And I recognise her

Come for my mother
Locked in her own
Immortal struggle
The sister returned
So I know it won't
Be long now

And I cry a little at
The unbearable beauty
Of these diastoles
When we are all
Suspended
Here in a heartbeat

Between heaven and earth

Inversion

She had always sparkled
My beautiful vivacious mother
Her irrepressible soul radiating out through every pore
Till we bore witness as time leached out of her
Betrayed by her own rogue code dismantling her cell by cell
And for a while she seemed to take everything inside

But in her end of days, she surrendered all opaqueness
Embracing a glass-eyed reflective transparency
Like a raindrop suspended, projecting
This glittering world it has captured
In that last precious pause
Before it

Falls

Transfusion

It had happened somewhere
Between birth and first steps
Subtly but all-consumingly

It was nothing she could give back
Even if
She had wanted to

It was there when she first found her voice
Surrendered
To her own wilfulness

Flew away and came back
Over and over
Through the years

It witnessed her hang on
As her mother
Passed away

Buoying her whenever
Her wings
Failed

Whispering possibilities
Swaying fears
Echoing her tears

How ever long since she'd left
The sea stayed
Forever

Pulsing through her veins
Constant and unquestionable
As the rise and fall

Of her heart

Gone

"She's gone"
She said
But I knew
She was wrong

I felt your gasp
At the sudden
Vast blackness
When she shut your lids

Your revolt
As she folded
Over the sheet
Your passing incomplete

I pulled it back
When she'd left
With her bits and bags
Whispered your name

The waves echoing
Over and over
The stories
We had shared

Fearless in concert
As we were now
Fingers tangled
Separate but inseparable

The warmth of your palm
Stubbornly
Denying her
Parting proclamation

* * *

I woke
To the screech
Of the sea-wind
Overrunning the window cracks

My head
Cradled in your lap
Your hand
Ice-cold in mine

And I knew
As I'd slept
She had won
I had let down your defences

You'd slipped away
From my slackened grip
Away
Across the waves

Past the hungry tide
Sucking at the shingle
Into the black
Still sky

Beyond the pane

Into the west

Wild white horses
Racing for shore
Come gather me up
I will stay here no more

Whisk me away
And turn on your heel
Into the west wind
Away let us steal

Wild white horses
Race me away
Over the shingle
I no more will stay

I've no use for earth
No more love of the land
Sweep me away now
Far from the strand

Carry me westward
Across the blue crests
Over the ocean
Till I find me some rest

The porpoises singing
Will lull me to sleep
And currents will rock me
As I yield to the deep

When the sun sets the day down
Sinking into the sea
The ocean on fire
Can remind you of me

Suspension

A robe suspended
A lipstick up-ended
A slipper askance
A curtain masking
A silent expanse

A form
A lip
A foot
A passing
Absolute

Love left hanging
For a year
Or more
Trickles to the
Waiting floor

Wayfare

A scattering of blue skies
A pocketful of hope
The love of a good man
No regrets
The promise of a world made miraculously less cruel for my children
Easy company
The smell of the sea

All that I desire
On the long walk home

Seagull dreaming

lean with me
                into the
                        wings of the wind

            and we'll fly
                   off the edge
                                of the world

                        adrift
            far above
      the waves

                throbbing
  with the thunder
      of a hundred hooves

        stirring softly-held
                  secrets from
                        the silver sands

                siren-song
                    floating
                        on the breeze

                  seasoned
              with the tang
    of a thousand tears

            way up high
              we can glide
                  aloof and untouchable

        sailing
             through the sky
                  slip into the light

                      gilded with its
                           endless
                              possibilities

Mirror, mirror in the hall

in the crook
of your elbow
over my shoulder

all these moments
of tiny kindnesses
stand

like a hall of
mirrors stretching
back through the years

all these tears
frozen
in time

I don't know
how to keep
a whole year
in a week

and each year
seems
so much longer
with each
passing week

while I stand
quietly soaking
the crook of
your elbow
over my shoulder

another welcome
home
melding into
another
year's
goodbye

Nowhere people

...when everyone's laughing
but you missed the start
because you came
from somewhere else

far away
that you left
too long ago
now to fit in

so when you go back
you're still the person
standing there staring
while everyone else is laughing

Year's end at Our Lady of Dolours

Molten gold shafts
Through a lofty oculus
Solemn words spill
From gathered mouths

The body broken
Blood mixes with water
A chalice passed
To drink our redemption

Black crows circle and swoop
Launching volleys at
The arched windows
Their raucous protest

Swallowed in the last strains
Of *O Holy Night*
As we bleed out
Into the shoppers' wake

Christmas kisses

We never had it
It was something you saw in the movies
old ones re-running on tv
that handsome couples
teasingly kissed under

Chaste tristes in black and white
like the pure white
berries of the mistletoe
But perhaps a bit waxen
Somewhat wooden

I remember my father laughingly
kissing my mother once
under a holly sprig
It seems more apt
So much more like love

with its pricks
and bright red shiny beads

Homing

A stranger now
In a strange land
This street my feet had pattered
Through all the years that mattered
In between the ghosts
Of fallen heroes
The smoke of burnt out fires
Monuments to the ruins
Of dreams and desires
Past facades masking
Tattered insides
All the laughing, skipping, dancing
Hauling, falling length of it
A street baptised in people's lives

A little street
In a little town
At the wave-washed edge
Of the world

Come and find me

where wailing walls
of moss-rolled stone
slowly yielding to a
centuried crusade
cling with smoke of long-gone
bog-fires now forever
married with the drifting
sea-mist lifting over
impossibly green fields
clutching ancient secrets
drop sharply off
to pitching shale
where swarming gulls rise
with the lagging tide
running the gusts
plunging with the lulls
to swoop and pull
a glistening haul
under the flagging watch
of a water-locked tower
marking the ethereal line
between sky and sea
and spectral hills loom
long past muted islands
still harbouring
a ship-wrecked shore

Come and find me
in the dying light
where a cormorant calls unanswered
shallow over his own ghost

Photograph: David Clare, First Light Photography

ANNE CASEY's poems have been published in *The Irish Times*, *The Murmur Journal*, *The Incubator*, *Other Terrain*, *Backstory*, *Into the Void Magazine*, *ROPES Literary Journal*, *The Remembered Arts Journal*, *Dodging the Rain*, *Tales from the Forest*, *Luminous Echoes: A Poetry Anthology*, *Deep Water Literary Journal*, *The Blue Nib*, *VisualVerse: An Anthology of Art and Words* and *Thank You For Swallowing*, among others.

Anne passionately believes that every poem, like all art, should leave you changed by the experience. Her poem, "In Memoriam II: The Draper," was the fifth most-read item – across all categories – in *The Irish Times* on the day of publication, and resulted in a furore of social media commentary.

She was shortlisted for the Cúirt New Writing Poetry Prize in 2017 and the Bangor Poetry Competition 2016. Originally from the west of Ireland, Anne lives in Australia. She has worked as a business journalist, magazine editor, corporate and government communications director, author and editor. Anne holds a Law degree and qualifications in Communications.

Website: www.anne-casey.com   Twitter: twitter.com/1annecasey